THE VOICE OF CONSCIOUSNESS

The Voice *of* Consciousness

Poems Composed After Ninety

Jack Rothman

TEBOT BACH • HUNTINGTON BEACH • CALIFORNIA • 2020

Dedicated to my wife, Judy

Companion and Helpmate Extraordinary

A Short Intro

I want to tell you a few things before you delve into my poems. This is a delayed harvest, about 95% of the poems germinated after age ninety. I've published many books of prose on community organizing, multiculturalism, filmmaking, and searching for my family's ancestral village. With time, I found that poetry became a more contracted, cogent way to express my thinking and feelings about what is important to me. I found the focus of poetry easier to work with than the wide scope of books I had written. My poems dig into the past, embrace the present, look to the future.

You will see that my poems are accessible, like low hanging fruit you can easily reach and digest. For many people, much of contemporary poetry is nebulous and abstract, a tussle for readers to comprehend. Friends asked me to write poems they can understand without struggle and bafflement. My poems are meant to suit the ordinary informed individual who enjoys reading, their depth and meaning apparent without having to track to the dictionary or Wikipedia. I hope these verses will bring pleasure to a wide audience, and with luck, help expand poetry from the smallish niche it has somehow slid into.

That said, enjoy the poems and come back for my next book.

—Jack Rothman

Contents

Musings

Family

Humor

Musings

Precious Consciousness

I wake up and sense my leg is itching
I hear a bird chirping outside my window
I feel the sun giving my forehead a warm bath
I worry about my echocardiogram report this afternoon
I have to call my accountant about that tax question
I smell my wife's perfect coffee drifting up the stairs
I awake immersed in consciousness
A unique, remarkable trait of human beings
A very special possession

Scientists in their sober journal writings
Hold that other creatures have consciousness
Unique and more limited
Missing awareness
Of a complex, convoluted self
Of morality
Of mortality
Of the sensation of existence in time and space
And of consciousness—itself
We humans are preoccupied with the language of consciousness
Self-conscious, pre-conscious, un-conscious, non-conscious

Consciousness is our very selves
The thought of losing it is inconceivable and terrifying
The thought of death is inconceivable and terrifying
It means the vanishing of our consciousness
Like at the end of a book
When the text finishes
There comes a blank flyleaf
The clear page tells us with its plain blankness
That the drama and poignancy of the narrative is over

Clever and sincere theologians and storefront preachers
Seek to allay our fears
They say we can be conscious in a future existence
High up, in the realm of heaven
We can be conscious there
As can our host of ancestors
And all other good and decent people who ever lived
Or we may be conscious in a reincarnated life
As a different version of ourselves

We can be rescued from the disappearance of consciousness
If we would only believe
Believe that we alone are divinely selected
Have powers consigned by a supernatural protector
A bestowal all other creatures are denied
Given to us by a protector or lord or savior
A consciousness granter
Who we are told looks like us
Although nobody has seen that hallowed figure

After I die, I'll go on having a survival of sorts
In this dominion
For a generation or two
In the consciousness of my children and grandchildren
And in the consciousness of others I have touched
Friends and neighbors
Decades of graduate students
My writings will go on informing and stirring readers
Including people I don't know
Or who haven't been born yet
That's a comforting truth to keep close

I'm past ninety now
My remaining calendar pages are few
And I will have to soon confront
The vanishing of my consciousness
That's the way of being
And of not being

So I want to be ready to say
Goodbye consciousness
Holding in my dread of your absence
You've been a constant companion
And a good one—mostly
And I will keep clutching to you firmly
Until I have to let you go.

A Struggle for Language

First an experience, a theme, an image
Then a mind blast to discharge a word flow
Searching for my best words
Vivid, allegorical, haunting
Building blocks for phrases and sentences
Banners that touch the heart and mind
That keep aloft my emerging song

Troubling specimens sprinkle willy-nilly
My literary scalpel trims
Shorter, more inventive, more tender, less tender
Delete, elongate, hyphenate, drop, relocate
Change the title/fix the meter
Until I say—that's it
That's me

       Hopefully inspiring readers to feel
       What they carry in their souls—
       Provoke them to join hands
       Perchance to cure the world
       Or at least have a needed chuckle

       I might instead spin out a puzzle
       To tease and perplex forever

The Cushion

The cushion sits serenely
Atop my wife's sewing machine
In our bedroom
Sitting there for months
Life's demands and diversions
Deter her beleaguered self
From darning the frayed seam
Tacking down dangling threads
Placing it in its normal spot
On a sofa in a corner of the living room

I pass it every day
The colors catch my eye
First the orange
Then the off-green
I think olive
Then the brown
A mellow fusion
The orange makes a statement
But not a loud one

The pattern resembles stripes
Irregular and impressionistic
Lines halt before reaching the other side
Wider on one end than the other
Originate on different sides of the cushion
Asymmetrical, unexpected, fittingly harmonic

These hues and their array
Sooth me every time I cross the room
Giving contentment and comfort
As I walk toward the bathroom
Or go the other way to descend the stairs

To rush to an appointment
Finally pick up the dry cleaning
Stop at the ATM for cash

The cushion awaits the impending repair
Unhurried and sunny on its perch
Radiating beauty where it sits
The two of us are bonding

I too display loose ends
I too need mending
And want repose
That fetching cushion
Has slowly become a mentor
To this wired resident
Teaching the worth of patience

Saying the Right Thing

Paula sat next to me
In the monthly poetry group
Neighboring strangers
She read her poem
About an old woman
She had seen through an open window
Dancing, alone, in the night
Like a siren or flower child
Like a young and spirited version of herself
And of Paula

Members of the group spoke
Fewer words—other words—a different slant
Paula held her ground
No changes
She showed a woman who knew herself
And what words were hers
Boldness contradicting her frail body

Back and forth it went
I voiced my view
I like it as it is

In the darkened parking lot
Going for our cars
She thanked me
Her bright, ample hat adorning her grateful face
We pulled out
In different directions
Into the vast space of L.A.

The next poetry group meeting
Our leader had a sad announcement
A shocking one
There was a mishap at the hospital
When Paula went in for something minor
Paula passed away
My mind shot back to the parking lot
Heard Paula's voice "You really get me—
I'm so glad when someone gets me"

How often do you come to know
In your stumbling way
You had said just the right thing?

Silent Subway Rides

At seventeen
Dating or call it non-dating
Words suffocated
Caught in my throat
Collapsed
Emerging as odd rumbles
Your shyness was no help
    Quiet
    Fearful
    Hiding
        Just like me

Taking your hand
Feeling distance and trepidation
Those silent rides on the subway
To a new downtown movie
Everyone and everything captivating
Absorbing
We weren't pressed
To fill empty time
Delivering words

Your black-haired beauty
Made me freeze
Was I worthy of this gift?
Would you take a plain guy
Inward
Tight
In the breeze of your dusky gorgeousness?
Blown over, blown away
Waiting for your reach
Watching for signals
Of acceptance or adoration
    That never came

Little Black Book

She wore a blue pants suit
Chuckled and teased me
No one uses those anymore
I pulled it back to my chest
My little black book
Making it obscure
Protecting it
The week-at-a-time calendar
Addresses and phone numbers
Pages for notes
My trusty information gatherer
Through most of my life

It shows its long-time service
Worn, torn
Scruffy, stuffed
Wrinkled pages
Coffee spots
These Filofax binders
Reliable and obliging
Since I landed my first job
Seventy years ago
This brand has stayed fixed and firm
From the time of its 1910 invention

When I require a new one
It's an identical twin
Keeping my life in order
Steering me to where
People expected me
Passing on unlisted numbers
When I was desperate
Never crashed

Or beseeched me to call a technician
That's what I told Ms. Pants Suit
Before lettering in
The time of our next meeting

    The current digital doodads
    Become passé
    In two years
    Obsolete
    Old fashioned
    Unprofitable
    To the Apple Company

But
For me
A little black book
Is forever

Poet's Block

Road Closed
Construction Ahead
My words are jammed
My fancy shuts down

How long do I strain
Before the route reopens
I take a break
Scatter my attention
Write checks
Apologize to my wife
Look out the window
Answer my emails
Tidy up the tattered photo album

With good fortune
The broom of random diversion
Sweeps the roadway clear
Fate extinguishes
The ugly *Road Closed* sign
And lo and behold—
Inspired construction ahead
The scaffolding for a poem

Inward Bound

I prized Dan Rubin
Sharp mind
Outspoken
Confident
A treasured professional colleague
Came from the original slums
Of Brownville in Brooklyn
He lived a hard life
Was a Golden Gloves boxer
Hauled himself up by his shredded bootstraps

Standing in a quiet corner
Of a noisy conference
I asked him about an off-center thesis
Been eking out for years
Would it fly
Or take heavy flak

My style
Caught his attention
You know, Jack
You don't have to please everyone
Don't have to be a nice guy
Something snapped
Drew me inward
Gave my mind a twirl

Even as a boy
I strained to please
Fair, Truthful, Accommodating
Molding my being to pristine values
Trailing a moral Northern Star
Being an upright specimen

But wasn't there also something else?

A Visit

So good of you to come
You volunteers are wonderful
Last time I thought it was my cousin Esther
Things are dull here
It's lonely
It's been a long time since my husband died
They tell me it was all of a sudden
Thanks for the cup of tea
I can manage the cup myself

I don't go for Bingo games and cards
Or staring into the TV
All Alzheimer's patients here
I used to be a teacher
Community College
Keep forgetting the name
Taught history
Loved FDR and the New Deal period
One of my former students came to visit
What a thrill
Someone told me he was here a few times
I like listening to the History Channel when it's on

The food isn't bad
Varies day by day
People are glued into their chairs
Some don't know how to dress
I wouldn't call this company
One night I forgot to turn off my room lights
Had a dreadful night's sleep
I didn't know why

It was wonderful to chat
Good-bye my dear

Food Connection

Think of Coney Island
The crowd in front of Nathan's Hot Dogs
From every conceivable niche of life
Together
On a common quest

    Talking about how hot it is
    How crowded
    Where they are from
    The mess on the subway cars
    Patient—for New Yorkers
    Contemplating a ride on the Cyclone
    Anticipating a dive into the rough waves
    Maybe a casual walk along the boardwalk
        Picking up a gorgeous chick

Food fills and intertwines them
In the passing instant
Then they evaporate
In the endless space of the city

Off Red

Painted on a newly constructed wall
Near the supermarket
Is an off-red
Middling and murky
A red that lulls
Rather than excites
A disappointment

Bold red catches my attention
Makes me brake at the street corner
It brashly calls STOP!
It could also be made to shout GO!
A striking red
Could give both orders
Befuddle everyone
Create an all-points quagmire
A glorious snarl

Would cause a time-out
When we could all come together
Hold a discussion
Propose a plan
To liberate us
From those jarring TV scenes
Every night
Broken politics and dumbed down culture
Brutal wars and cruel migrations
Tweets and Trumpisms

A red angry shade appears
That glares into history
Critically inspects
Our long lingering wrongs

Which are a mélange of injustices

                Slavery
                                        Native American Genocide

                        Japanese American internment

        Mexican Annexation
                                Latino injustices

                Gender transgressions

                                        Workers' rights denied

Our founders' ideals
Subverted
Their dreams
Of rebellion and change and equality
A vibrant red
Blood red
Now mingled with the blood of victims
And their defenders
A red that seeps to the roots
Of our fault lines
And strikes at
The lords of privilege
The complacent
The ignorant
A red that is resolute
To make America
Great
        At last

The Afghanistan Story

Afghanistan, Afghanistan
The British ran
The Russians ran
Then Al Qaeda ran
To regroup in Pakistan

What is the plan
Of the Donald man
For Afghanistan?
To ban
If he can
The Taliban?

They're a clan
The Pathan
Rooted in Afghanistan
Before the state began
And are no fan
Of that American
The Donald man

When will the Donald man
Finally be an also ran?

Seeing Peace

Oh, say can you see
Through dawn's hazy light
The missiles streaming in air
Our nukes still there
Over 800 military bases
In seventy countries
Around the globe
Sea to shining sea

America, America
    Padlock your bases
Return your brave soldiers
    Snuff out imperialism's great flare
Scrap the military-industrial mortuary
    Forsake forever war
From the mountains to the prairies to the oceans

America, America
Pause
Recalculate
And over the ramparts
Release a million white doves

Renewal

The word renewal
Sets off sparks in my mind
Multi-colored pinwheels
The excitement of life's prizes
A patient at the hospital door
Leaving after discharge
Ghetto kid with arms aloft
Holding his acceptance to Stanford
A frosted bottle of coke
After a long midsummer hike
Wooden beams of low-cost housing
Rising on a barren lot
My wife consumed with grace
Telling me she excuses me
Wherever I look there is renewal
Passing the high school today
Hundreds of students
Chant
Carrying posters
Demanding climate change action
Speaking hope amidst the waste

Lifestream

Turning backward, I see a rock-strewn stream, winding and tumbling down
    knolls
and sauntering along meadows.

The stream and my life comingle, for I have flowed nine decades and
    continue
to course, now at a decelerated pace.

I have reckoned with variation, irregularity, incongruity—the unpredictability
    of life.
What was the strange and perplexing, I now weave into a patchwork quilt of
    boundless normality.

Expect anything, I will tell my grandchildren--have patience and openness for
    oddities
in people and the drifts of life.

As a stream ambles, a thunderstorm ahead, so are we beings without clue
    of what awaits us.

Humankind is sunlight dancing on ripples of a stream—fluctuating and
    glittering haphazardly, new forms and colors appearing as others flow
    from sight.

Consider, for some, *you* are a rare, curious shape, an indistinct lifestream,
    rambling
and erratic, as you cross the landscape of human geography.

And know that none of what I say stands as stone, for just as a river runs
        from
    the heights to the sea carving out its watery reality, each of us hones our
        own truths and destinations in separate, mysterious ways.

Family

Manchild Portrait

I'm a montage
Many layers, many roles
Helping my wife do the dishes
Taking my children on a hike
Reading a story to my grandkids
Advising graduate students on their dissertations
Finishing writing a new book
(I've done a whole shelf of them)
You could have seen me traveling
In many cities here and overseas
Visiting museums and walking neighborhoods
Sometimes giving lectures
Sometimes doing book tours
You might have caught me
Doing a stand-up gig at a comedy club

Organization builder and policy shaper
Straining to mend the world
The walls of my study are filled
Gold-edged certificates, plaques, awards
"Outstanding Lifetime Achievement"
Did you spot me at a Broadway play?
Near the front row
Hearing aids capturing the words
That was me at the supermarket
Buying the family's groceries
At a protest rally
Holding an anti-war banner
And at the playground
Pushing my grandson
Endlessly on a swing

At core I'm a little boy
Two-years old
Mother stolen by cancer
Me abandoned and set aside
Bewildered
In a vast, threatening world
That my unshaped brain couldn't grasp
Frozen in a landscape of forsakenness
Indelibly branded "a reject"

Even now
Decade upon decade after
Through large tracts of time
I'm that infant child
Alone and vulnerable
Waiting for someone to pick me up

1935 A Day in August

AM

Pop, an immigrant ,
Owns a candy store
Somewhat shabby and worn
On a street corner in Queens
I sit at the marble counter
Cooling off with a vanilla milkshake
And read the new comic books
Before sneaking a girlie magazine to the back
Pop reminds me to dust the display cases
Holding candy and toys
A profusion of Shirley Temple dolls
A kid of eight can kill copious time
Taking in these distractions

Always a hard worker
The Great Wall Street Crash
Battered Pop's life
In a double disaster
He lost his wife the same year
And I a toddler of two
Lost my mother

Pop stretched to make a living
Enticed customers into the store
With Breyers ice cream
The best brand to him
Though it cost more pennies per gallon
Zealously enterprising
A pinball machine stood at a side wall
Where young men shoved nickels
Into a slot
Though illegal to gamble in New York

Pop slipped cash to high scorers
To lure more players
And scoop up extra nickels

PM

I am trying out a new toy wagon
Look up
Three brawny men edge into the store
One in a NYC policeman's blue uniform
New York's Finest
They wave Pop to the back of the store
I stare
What's happening/what's happening
Arms flap/talk intense
The words *betting* and *against the law*
Hover in the candy store air

A bulky plainclothesman
Clutches my father's arm
Steers him to the front door
I make a dash
Thrash this monster with frantic fists
Bellowing and bawling
As if in a trance
He pushing me away with one arm
I vault back at him
The cop barks at my father
You know you got a nervy kid

What *he* didn't know
Is I lost my mother
A few years before
And I would do anything
Against all obstacles
Not also to lose my father

Remembering Pop

Pop trudges the stairs wearily
each step is a challenge—
and painful victory.
From my bed I see the clock
on the bedroom bureau
as it ticks onward,
its scarecrow arms
proclaiming one o'clock.
The hushed streets in the silent city
lay still and sleep
in the dark night
while the creak of each stair
groans out its protest
through every room in the apartment.

Pop takes off his white linen jacket
sketched upon
with the pigments of his trade—
sticky chocolate syrup,
ice cream and the turgid air
of the city.
Pop seems smaller to me,
looks thinner than I remember,
working today as every day
in the candy store downstairs
that has devoured his years,
chewing a life
and giving back little in return.

He washes the sediment of the city off,
chews on a refrigerator leftover,
sips a glass of Swee-Touch Nee tea
and lifts the day's newspaper

softly, with affection.
His eyes play on the thrilling words
with effort.
The words do not sing out for him
for Pop is not an educated man
as are today's young men
in designer jeans
and trimmed beards,
and the very latest digital machine in hand.

Pop was sent to work at thirteen.
At fourteen he walked ten miles
to the flour mill where he carried
and weighed and recorded the sacks.
On Saturday night, he counted
and hid away
the rubles
that would free him from the Czar
who told him he could not own land
or live in the city
or have a profession
or be a man
but that he must buy and sell
and submit to the terror of the pogrom
when the Russian economy became sick.

He was told
the saved rubles
would deliver him to a land
where all people were equal
and where there was opportunity
and boundless wealth
for the honest man
who was not afraid to work.
Pop embraced the work

and hadn't the chance to learn
as I, his son, did
in the stilted and sullen New York City public schools
of bygone days.

Pop relaxes now.
His lips smile
and his tired eyes look happy
as they envelop the words and paragraphs
in the long columns
while his lids sink slowly.
And Pop nods and wakes and reads again.
And then it is time to sleep.

A restless sleep it will be,
a sleep that will be pierced
by the smug, ugly alarm clock
at six in the morning.
He tosses this way and that
his mind lingering over what he has read
of the laboring miner in South Africa
and of the peasant in Bolivia
and Pop worries about the struggling plantation worker
In Malaysia
and the fisherman on the Portuguese wharf.
He has even come to have compassion
for our own black people,
for the "schvartzes"
who fed the coal furnaces
in the dark cellars
on our block.

Pop is contented
as he feels the ties
with his fellow men

who dot the earth.
And he stretches,
sensing the tenderness
that flows through his tired frame,
the love for all the good people
which will bring him kinship and fortitude
when the candy store calls early
for him to start the grind
another day.

Bubba's Black Bread

Bubba called me for a treat
Between meals
Her long black shawl suggested she was
From Russia, or Poland, or the Ukraine
As a surrogate mother
She moved in with us
A few years before
In the Jewish quarter of Brownsville in Brooklyn
A four-year-old boy was a handful
At grandmother's age
But we were great pals
She showed me how to tie my shoes
And I showed her which trolleys to get on
When I learned to read the route signs

Bubba cut a thick slice of Russian black bread
With a dense, hard crust that must have been made of stones
She found on the disorderly streets
Of the Brownsville slum
She rubbed the crust fiercely with garlic
Her beloved "knobble"
Until the clove merged with the crust
Then slathered a side with deep yellow chicken fat
Heavy schmaltz
Who could count the layers?
A rain of thick Kosher salt was the finishing touch
All the flavors fusing

What a treat
I loved it
The garlic and schmaltz mix delivered a potent, one-of-a kind taste
Chicken fat softened the stiff bread to create a gooey texture
I needed a trove of napkins to fix my face

My young digestive tract
Had not yet come to relish one fare over another
My taste buds had not yet learned about social norms
That usher people to foods
Acceptable for mannered folk to eat

Sally and our Family's Escape

Cousin Sally, born in the family shtetl,
Western Ukraine near Kiev,
spoke of the turmoil and terror
that night, as a child of eight,
when the family was driven from their village
of Butsnevits. Maddened Cossacks
out on a pogrom during the Russian Civil War
raided her home in a ranting rage
searching for despised Jews.
Looting and lusting. A sword slashed
the arm of her defying mother.

Daybreak, the stolid matriarch Bubba
gathered her clan of six, the last
remaining family in this treacherous land.
Quickly they towed loved possessions
to a horse-driven cart, every precious belonging
shoehorned into a wobbly wagon,
and dashed to the Romanian border.

Ahead the Carpathian Mountains
Loomed like a forbidding enclosure
in the night, etched by falling snow.
Uniformed guards exacted sweet bribes.
The yearning for safety, impossible
as it seemed, propelled this fragile band
over the heights.

A half-century later, Sally speaks
about the ship in Hamburg, mammoth
to her child eyes. In squalid steerage
she remembers how the tossing swell
whirled her stomach, a diet of sardines

the only fare that held down.
Her mother, seasick in early pregnancy,
suffered the month-long journey.

With promise of a fresh life ahead
in America's refuge of freedom
and protection, spirits were high.
Her cherished mother carried within,
her new baby brother. Sally experienced
her first orange, savoring the nectar.

Andrew Dancing

Andrew is dancing.
Almost two-years-old, his legs pump up and down
In perfect time to the music.
As he twirls—joyfully with abandon—
I look with a grandfather's astonishment.

He lifts himself onto the coffee table,
Boldly treads its contour
Like a self-assured tightrope walker
Looking for new challenges to test his daring.
He starts to dance again
Near the edge.

Soon he walks to where I am standing,
Taking my index finger in hand
Leading me into the living room
Where the multi-colored blow up ball was left.
Like soccer champs,
We are out to win the gold cup,
Again.

Outside In the distance, a fire engine's wail pierces
The privacy of our match,
Whooping, undulating, ever louder, as it passes by.
Andrew rushes to me
Puts his arms around my thighs,
His face radiating concern and fright
Until the ghostly siren slowly fades away.
We are silent for a time
Clinging to one another.

In the family room Andrew's mother
Plays a new Barney video, music rises up,
And Andrew is dancing again.
His chunky legs moving in harmony with the beat,
Animated and cocky in his gyrations
As though this moment is always.

That Room

That room
Between my bedroom and my father's
Always dim
No windows
Dim

Shabby bureaus and cabinets
Scuffed and scratched
Brought from the Czar's Russia
Or the Lower East Side
Old china and tarnished utensils
A mottled hairbrush and pearl-handled mirror
From when my mother was alive
From before her death when I was two

Spooks jumped out at me
Goblins, ghosts and monsters
Dark and murky green
Like I saw at the movie house across the street
That room
Converging into a nightmare
And a haunted house
I ran through fast
Every time
So the spooks wouldn't scoop me up

Passing over decades
To my daughters house
In a before-bed snuggle
My grandson confided
Fear of his bedroom at night
Things lurk and menace
I told him not to worry
In time those thoughts go away
Don't they?

At Amy's

My daughter's house
Is a celebration
Her two pups appear
Barking up a frantic welcome
Massaging my legs with their paws
Until they decide
I've petted them enough
My grandson Andrew appears
Inches taller
With a body-crunching hug
That ends too soon

I see the spacious kitchen
With a long wooden table
For eating
And lingering family chats
At Thanksgiving
Or Father's Day
Amy's dishes are creations
Of splendor and taste
That beckon me to return
Before long

I see her hovering
Over a skillet
Stirring her incomparable
Browned Brussels sprouts
She admires my new sweater
Complains about Andrew
Never straightens his room
Asks me if I would like a glass of wine

She is a sprite in the kitchen
Shuffling pots and pans
Effortlessly
With grace and ease
A natural force in her terrain
Her steps moving nimbly to the beat
Of her singular drummer

Stepping into the outside patio
A blast of sunshine and color
Dazzle my vision
Green intertwined vines
A band of red flowers
Lemon trees
And a stately white birch
Straining to reach even higher

Cushioned chairs cluster
In the shadow of Amy's tree
Draw me to idle tranquility
Under the timeless sky

Thanksgiving Thoughts

Thanksgiving is for family
A time to overcome distance
Personal and geographic
The table brimming with food
My wife's cranberry sauce
A fitting companion
For the turkey
Deep red in hue
Taste between tart and sweet
Laced with cinnamon sticks and oranges
Consistency between loose and firm
This merging of disparities
A magical force
For molding camaraderie

And for us
Late that night
A midnight snack
When we review
With wonderment and gladness
The communion
On this day
Wishing it was not
So fleeting

The Smell of Houses

A sinus nemesis
Cramped my nasal powers
I respond to alternatives

The smell of my house
Is comfort
Watercolor paintings on the walls
Some by my wife
Colors co-mingle throughout the rooms
Oak wood paneling imparts mellow
The lounge chairs and sofas speak ease
An imaginative architect
Planted affable alcoves about
For secluded chats

Our furniture is vintage
Mid-century Scandinavian
Each piece bought new
When we wed
They have silently morphed into antiques
As have we
In age but not in essence

Come and visit
Smell the comfort and congeniality of our house
And talk to us about yours

On the Steps

My wife and I together
Mount the steps
Of time
Her hand giving me support
To coax my ailing hip
She is 87
I am older
The steps seem steeper

She walks slower now
Bends softly
I saw her trip yesterday
That didn't used to happen
She is a non-complainer
Strictly
Yet told me this morning
Her shoulder aches
Maybe arthritis
Her leg hurts at night
Maybe a carryover from sciatica
And she forgot where she left
The instruction sheet from the doctor
Very rare

She is a composite
A young persona prevails
With Verve
Inquisitiveness
Resourcefulness
Humor
Tempered by the late night visitation
Of a silent old woman

Liver

My stepmother
An eccentric and rigid woman
Made the same dinner
Every night of the week
Salmon on Monday nights
Each Tuesday was flank steak
Wednesday night was a horror
Always thick liver
Undercooked
Rubbery
Gluey
A dish sent by the devil
To torture small boys

My wife is a liver lover
She slips the dish on the table now and then
To trick
Or surprise me
Surprise me she did
Making it in an dissimilar fashion
Thin cut
Cooked through
Drowning in elegant sautéed onions
That Imposed their own flavor and fragrance

Who would have predicted
I would go to the kitchen
Sidle up to my wife
Put my arm around her waist
And propose straight out
Honey, how about liver tomorrow night?

My Wife's Scarves

She has many
A profusion of colors
Today we chose a light gray one
With tiny squares in bright shades
At the Hammer Museum gift shop

I am taken by the miniature hues
Those accents in purple and red
Jousting with her pure white hair
This scarf has varied patterns
Round, stripes, zigzags, splattered

Her scarves need to be short
Lightweight and airy
Not irritating her skin
Not eclipsing her smallish dimensions
Tied in a square knot
Or hanging loosely
Where they imitate her spirited pace

Whichever one she picks to wear
She walks in beauty

New Shoes

My father would tell me
Time for new shoes
Your sneakers are *farkakt*
Yiddish slang for
They look shitty
Pop was also Mom
Filling an empty slot as a widower
He took time from his pressing candy store
To walk me down Myrtle Avenue
A business street where trolley cars rattled
To a block where three shoe stores clustered

We peered into their windows
Saw a pair I thought looked swell
Blue with thick white laces
Pop had eyes for practical, cheap, and roomy
Shoes I could grow into until fifth grade
We always got Keds
My father—the salesman—a woman customer
Their eternity of fingers poked my toes
I tried on different sizes
Walked the length of the store and back
A done deal
The ornate bronze cash register rang up the sale

Bolting out of the store
I ran up Myrtle Avenue
To our apartment above the candy store
Skipping, springing, and soaring all the way
Good prep for a pickup basketball game
In the schoolyard behind PS 77 Queens

Those memories as sweet as
The Baby Ruth candy bars
Kids lined up to buy

I've since used and discarded
A legion of calendars
Aging has chiseled my body
According to its willful plan
Arthritis has invaded my joints
My energy rises but soon plummets
My father would call me an *alta cocker*

I never skip now
Or spring
No matter what shoes I wear

Ode to My Miata

When I pull into my garage
The dimly lit space beneath our house
There is the empty spot where it used to rest
My sleek, silver Miata convertible
Bought twenty-eight years before
Among the original off the assembly line
I held on to it
Despite my wife's unease about safety
And the wind's ravaging of her hair

My Miata remained streamlined and sporty
Ever youthful
As I sprouted signs of aging
A perfect vehicle in my Los Angeles refuge
From the icy frost of Michigan winters
My sweet Miata allowed me to embrace
The clement climate and sunshine
Its open contour erased boundaries
Its manual shift aligned me with the motor
And the wheels turned on a sliver of a dime
This was an old man's toy
That generously also bestowed transport

Time changed the game
My ancient bones and joints
Protested lifting my body from the low seats
Demanded a sedan
With raised seats
That do not challenge impaired hips
They pressed me to resign my ownership

I taught my teenage grandson
How to drive and shift gears
In the huge empty lot
Behind the VA Hospital
Andrew adored driving a stick shift
He dug the cool apparatus
Wanted to go on taking lessons
In this shimmering machine
Long after he was proficient

My physical change
Called for vehicular change
I gave a gift to Andrew
An heirloom
He did not expect
He now navigates the Miata
With the care and love
That I had bestowed on it
Leaning on my cane
I see a glint on the horizon
An auto and a young man
Flowing along the Southern California sunset

Humor

My Gateway to Poetry

My poetry springs from the comic
I was born with a funny bone
Or was it many funny bones
I've merged humor and poetry
When still a kid
Ogden Nash tickled me
Made me laugh more than comic books
I chuckled at the wisdom of his wit
A child need not be very clever
To learn that 'Later, dear' means 'Never.'

I put my own droll thoughts
Into rhyme
Prodded by family events
I gave a lift to birthday parties
People admired my ditties
Cheering me on
To inflict more on them
Even up to a recent birthday
Here I am at eighty-eight
Not yet at the Pearly Gate
Everyone knows I'm always late
Saint Peter simply has to wait

My poems morphed over time
Free verse supplanting rhyme
(Not entirely)
Musings join the amusings
My humble beginnings
Have led to a humble ending
In my jocular poetry career

Humor hasn't the panache
In the world of poetry
As does dire profundity

When matched with Browning and Yeats
Nash falls short amidst these greats
Nash you see is not on par
So pardon while I find a bar

The Fly

Tiny is the common fly
Its wingspan miniscule
Beside the eagle
But "fly" can expand
Has scope
Intrudes indiscriminately

Airplanes fly
And flags
Capricious businesses fly by night
A fly in the ointment
Can rattle your life
Fly right to straighten up
A boxed in wife can fly the coop
Or go on the fly
People win with flying colors
Fly off the handle if they lose
A gadfly flitters
Annoying people
Just like a real fly
Rumors fly
My trousers have one

A poem can fly
Soar and explore
You can end a conversation with
Gotta fly
And also a poem

[Dedicated to the Spirit of Ogden Nash]

Busy

This'll be short
Because I'm busy
Everyone is busy
The breeze of busyness
Is blowing everywhere
  Gotta run

  Deadlines that keep us up
  Traffic jams that hold us down
  Whooshing kids to afterschool programs
  Dashing to CVS before it closes
  Changing passwords, remembering passwords
  Email, iPhone, Facebook, tweets
  Once at the office
  Now in my home

This country is a democracy
But we've not had a chance to vote
At the ballot box
Secretly
On whether we want to be so busy

  Gotta Run!

Voting

The citizens have voted; they've cast their lot
We're sure they voted, who knows for what?
They vote to the left, then switch to the right
On what they believe, they shed little light

The poll results, they're not worth a nickel—
We pick our leaders in ways that are fickle
Elect a scoundrel, the next time a cad
Whoever can pay for a cool TV ad

The right is united; decisions don't drag
In every election they vote for the flag
The left is inept but remarkably pure
Maiming each other on matters obscure

Health care reform, that's a socialist plot
Global warming, the earth's not that hot
The infrastructure, don't add a new tax
The mentally ill, should learn to relax

I hate to be pinned with the label *elite*
But I'm ready now to withstand the heat
On this they tell me I ought to keep mum
The voting public is plain friggn' dumb

Courtesy Past

People spoke kind words
Stopped to ask about health and family
Begged your pardon
Held the door open for old folks
Followed the natural laws of courtesy
Abruptly the phrases of courtesy
Became supplanted by a distinct word
Hurled while I'm waiting
At the bus stop

A hulking millennial dashes by
Pushes me aside and bellows
Asshole
Omnipresent
The lingua franca of now
Have we become a nation
Of proctologists?

Have a nice day!

The Stain

My wife saw it
At breakfast
On my left pant leg
A thin black streak
From when I placed my bike on the rack
Of my old silver Miata
To drive to the Santa Monica bike path
Where the ocean breeze
Gives my face
A cool morning massage

A different stain today than yesterday
I don't see them
My mind ruminates
About yesterday, tomorrow, no-time
A lecture I have to prepare for class
That new screw up by Congress
My visit to the cardiologist
My son's bid on a new house
Will I remember to stop at the bank?
Will I master that new fiddly app?
Will the dean approve my sabbatical?

All along the way
My thin skin spawns
A million injuries to brood about
Worries—plans—preoccupations
Leave little open space in my brain
To perceive the palpable world
Dancing around me

Stains are trivial to me
Invisible
For my wife
Who observes all
And then tends to all
Those spots besmirch her image
They are an elephant in the room

In my life
A stain is a strain

And a spot counts a lot

Monkey Talk

At the Los Angeles Zoo
In Griffith Park
I gaze a long time at our forerunners
Who swing through trees
Like seasoned entertainers
Spin with abandon on ropes
Tumble jubilantly through hanging tires

I love how they stare back
Through iron bars
Fire an impish spitball
And pick at each other in high camp
Squealing loudly as if delighted
Or having a panic attack
Scrambling down a wall upside down

Indelicately they devour
A whopping bunch of bananas
And babble jumbled dialogue
Channeling stand-up comics

Oh to be a monkey
And make all the world laugh

America Ain't Got No Social Classes

I've seen hard times between my flings
And heard a lot of quirky things
But one of all sure tops my list
Of myths that soon should be dismissed.

On every channel on every screen
The US comes off squeaky clean
Is that the poor the news bypasses?
"America ain't got no social classes."

I've seen the low and seen the high
From Walnut Creek to Bedford Stuy
Yet schoolbooks tell our trodden masses
"America ain't got no social classes."

The barrio dines on the day's remains
While Wall Street gobbles capital gains
Still word goes out to lads and lasses
"America ain't got no social classes."

Our Congress holds a slew of sages
Who have no clue on workers' wages
They talk in tongues and discharge gases
"America ain't got no social classes."

Corporate heads use tweets and faxes
To moan the weight of crushing taxes
They think we're all a bunch of asses
"America ain't got no social classes."

From the hills in swank Bel Air
They cry out regs are so unfair
Their anguished groans show what crass is
"America ain't got no social classes."

The 1%'s a grubbing crew
We know what we've got to do
No matter how the right harasses
Lets create more equal classes!

The 1%

We're the 1% of Wall Street fame
We run the sleezy finance game.

A subprime mortgage is what you chose
We sadly made your house foreclose.

You're down and out, you're tied in knots
That news is nil out on our yachts.

The famous buyout had a sequel
This land became big-deal unequal.

We hold the reins, don't you knock it
Congress sits neatly in our pocket.

Money and power—ours for the keeping
Too bad Lady Liberty's weeping.

Don't wring your hands and yell "unfair"
Our pal, the Hidden Hand, won't care.

The hand moves on, not to linger
Set to give poor folks the finger.

The Donald

Donald each day tweets a torrent of words
But tweeting, you know, is meant *for the birds*

Most of the words are reckless and crude
So why are the media totally glued?

He struts and boasts with never a halt
Neglecting achievements in sexual assault

Self-exhibition's a passion that burns
Except when it comes to his tax returns

The GOP fought for his tax bill to pass
Giving generous doles to the billionaire class

His health plan exudes a conservative creed
Shafting the poor who have medical need

Health care regs protect peoples' fate
Trump never saw one that he didn't hate

Mental health services he decimates, sadly
Just what his supporters need so badly

Fairness for whites is his deep obsession
Rejecting "fake news" on racial oppression

His brash bravado an empty flare
Fumbling through the pandemic scare

Pack his bags and show him the gate
That's the way to make America Great

Farewell Trump—back to your Tower
Time for the sane to exercise power

About Yellow

A color soothing, easy on the eyes
But a coward?
The luminous lift of yellow
Expresses valiance
Yellow Jacket bees with their potent sting
The yellow surge of sunflowers rising
To almost touch the golden sun
Whose brilliant beams invade
Tenement hallways and abandoned barns
The yellow jackets of first responders
The yellow vests of social protest—
A radiant gleam

April 1 Today

My grandson Andrew is twenty-one, a new age
and world for him. He has a girlfriend, a car,
a nice apartment and job as a software engineer,
senior rank, making more money than I did
when I retired. Very private, he is inward
and self-contained etching his path to adulthood.

Should I continue my April Fools' pranks?
A tradition since his boyhood? YES!
I text him:
> *I just read that they made a mistake about the millennium*
> computer blackout. New calculations show it will take place
> in 2019—right after April Fools' Day.

Will he reply?
Get in the spirit?
Find it an affront to his maturity?

His response is the answer:
> *I knew you would do something funny. But you're actually*
> not too far off. A Scientific group predicts computers
> will stop working on the 19th of January, 2038.

And he added—
> Were you able to prank grandma?
I told him I didn't. He replied—

> No prank is the biggest prank.

Nobody's fool, Andrew is still Andrew!

An Elusive Blue

She handed me the swatch
Deep blue
Sky blue
A thin mesh fabric
Plays tricks on my eyes
Twist it and it becomes lighter
Role it and it becomes darker
Place it on top of another color
It absorbs it
Ingests lines and shapes
And becomes them

This blue swatch
I want to describe
Is infinitely fungible
And nondescript...
Light as a feather
Wily as a chameleon
Transparent as a link fence
Variable as a weather vane

My Yellow Pencil

A buddy
For as long as I can remember
Gives me confidence and purpose
Confidence boosted by a sturdy eraser
I make jottings
Pick up soda at the supermarket
Remember to get the dry cleaning
Call State Farm about the fender bender
The pencil isn't only practical
That bent old man
Prompts a note for a poem
As does the trashed red truck
Abandoned on the street corner
My yellow pencil may be worn out
The eraser a stump
Just give us a little more time
And we'll compose
A lasting anniversary rhyme
For my wife

Stereotypic Couple

Suddenly I notice a door
Never seen before
Down the street
A dull brown hue
Leading to a soggy cellar
With ancient clutter
Or a hoard of diamonds
Difficult to know

It happens often
My mind overloaded
With trivia and gravitas
Will there be enough Cheerios for breakfast
Will my stress test come out OK this afternoon

I haven't noticed
The door to wealth
Or the one to celebrity
I don't spot what floor it is
When the elevator halts
Ending up at the wrong landing
I miss a STOP sign
When driving home
Don't spy a police car following me

My wife offsets my lack
We channel a stereotypic couple
I focus on society
Unraveling political quandaries
She monitors our surroundings
A broken chair or leaky faucet
Will not escape correction for very long

I am mending the world
She is mending our household
Truth to tell
She is more successful—

That I *have* noticed

Acknowledgments

Thanks is given to the editors of the *Huffington Post* for originally releasing three of the poems, in different versions: "The 1%", "The Afghanistan Story" and "Voting"

As a new poet at an advanced age, I was at ill ease about my ability to change successfully from a long career of prose writing to verse form. Enthusiastic supporters gave me the determination to push forward. Deborah Clayton, teacher of a poetry class at OASIS Lifelong Adventure in Santa Monica, marked me legitimate in an authoritative and befriending way. Michael Powell robustly admired my work in a group of poets who met weekly to read and critique each other's writings at Beyond Baroque Literary Arts Center in Los Angeles. My editor, Perie Longo of Santa Barbara, was supremely proficient, congenial, and always laudatory. From the very beginning, my wife Judy was my right-off-the-printer editor, as well as stalwart booster and guide. To all of them, my grateful thanks for helping get me to this place.

About the Author

75

Jack Rothman has written extensively on social change and community organizing. He has authored twenty-five books, *The Voice of Consciousness* his first poetry collection. He has contributed to *Huffington Post*, the *Nation*, *Social Policy*, and the *Humanist*. Rothman is a professor emeritus at UCLA and a member of the Beyond Baroque Poetry Center. He has been a stand-up comic at comedy clubs and coffee houses in Los Angeles and an avid cyclist on the Santa Monica bike path. If you visit his home, don't miss looking at his grand collection of novelty bottle openers. He is married, has three children and two grandchildren, and lives in Los Angeles.

TEBOT BACH
A 501 (c) (3) Literary Arts Education Non Profit

THE TEBOT BACH MISSION: advancing literacy, strengthening
community, and transforming life experiences with the power of poetry
through readings, workshops, and publications.

THE TEBOT BACH PROGRAMS
1. A poetry reading and writing workshop series for venues such as homeless
shelters, battered women's shelters, nursing homes, senior citizen daycare
centers, Veterans organizations, hospitals, AIDS hospices, correctional
facilities which serve under-represented populations. Participating poets
include: John Balaban, Brendan Constantine, Megan Doherty, Richard Jones,
Dorianne Laux, M.L. Leibler, Laurence Lieberman, Carol Moldaw, Patricia
Smith, Arthur Sze, Carine Topal, Cecilia Woloch.

2. A poetry reading and writing workshop series for the community Southern
California at large, and for schools K-University. The workshops feature
local, national, and international teaching poets; David St. John, Charles
Webb, Wanda Coleman, Amy Gerstler, Patricia Smith, Holly Prado, Dorothy
Lux, Rebecca Seiferle, Suzanne Lummis, Michael Datcher, B.H. Fairchild,
Cecilia Woloch, Chris Abani, Laurel Ann Bogen, Sam Hamill, David Lehman,
Christopher Buckley, Mark Doty.

3. A publishing component to give local, national, and international poets a
venue for publishing and distribution.

Tebot Bach
Box 7887
Huntington Beach, CA 92615-7887
714-968-0905
www.tebotbach.org